First World War
and Army of Occupation
War Diary
France, Belgium and Germany

39 DIVISION
Divisional Troops
184 Brigade Royal Field Artillery
4 February 1916 - 30 November 1916

WO95/2574/4

The Naval & Military Press Ltd
www.nmarchive.com
Published in association with The National Archives

Published by

The Naval & Military Press Ltd

Unit 10 Ridgewood Industrial Park,

Uckfield, East Sussex,

TN22 5QE England

Tel: +44 (0) 1825 749494

www.naval-military-press.com

www.nmarchive.com

This diary has been reprinted in facsimile from the original. Any imperfections are inevitably reproduced and the quality may fall short of modern type and cartographic standards.

© **Crown Copyright**
Images reproduced by permission of The National Archives, London, England, 2015.

Contents

Document type	Place/Title	Date From	Date To
Heading	WO95/2574 Mar 16-Nov 16 184 Bde RFA		
Heading	184th Brigade R.F.A. Mar 1916-Nov 1916		
Heading	184th Brigade Royal Field Artillery 4.2.16 To 31st March 1916		
Miscellaneous	184 R F A Vol I		
War Diary			
War Diary	Milford	04/02/1916	02/03/1916
War Diary	Southampton	06/03/1916	06/03/1916
War Diary	Havre	07/03/1916	08/03/1916
War Diary	Thiennes	09/03/1916	09/03/1916
War Diary	Blaringhem	10/03/1916	10/03/1916
War Diary	Steenwerck	12/03/1916	12/03/1916
War Diary	Croix-Du-Bac	13/03/1916	13/03/1916
War Diary	Armenties	14/03/1916	14/03/1916
War Diary	Steenwerck	19/03/1916	19/03/1916
War Diary	Armenties	20/03/1916	24/03/1916
War Diary	Estaires	25/03/1916	25/03/1916
War Diary	Armenties	23/03/1916	23/03/1916
War Diary	St Venant	25/03/1916	31/03/1916
Heading	184th Brigade Royal Field Artillery April 1916		
War Diary	St Venant	01/04/1916	14/04/1916
War Diary	Locon	16/04/1916	16/04/1916
War Diary	Givenchy	17/04/1916	28/04/1916
Heading	184th Brigade Royal Field Artillery May 1916		
War Diary	Essars	01/05/1916	03/05/1916
War Diary	Locon	05/05/1916	05/05/1916
War Diary	Givenchy	12/05/1916	23/05/1916
War Diary	Locon	25/05/1916	28/05/1916
Heading	184th Brigade Royal Field Artillery June 1916		
War Diary	Locon	01/06/1916	20/06/1916
War Diary	Fosse	20/06/1916	30/06/1916
Heading	184th Brigade Royal Field Artillery July 1916		
Heading	War Diary Of 184th Brigade. R.F.A. from 1st July 1916 to 31st July 1916 (Volume 1)		
War Diary	La Fosse	06/07/1916	06/07/1916
War Diary	Bethune	09/07/1916	11/07/1916
War Diary	La Perol	11/07/1916	24/07/1916
Heading	184th Brigade Royal Field Artillery August 1916		
Heading	War Diary Of 184th Brigade R.F.A. From 29/7/16 To 26/8/16 (Volume 1)		
War Diary	Le Perol	29/07/1916	11/08/1916
War Diary	Ames	12/08/1916	12/08/1916
War Diary	Rollecourt	13/08/1916	21/08/1916
War Diary	Grouches	22/08/1916	22/08/1916
War Diary	Sarton	25/08/1916	26/08/1916
Miscellaneous	39th Divisional Artillery Order No. 31	26/08/1916	26/08/1916
Heading	184th Brigade Royal Field Artillery September 1916		
Heading	War Diary Of 184th Brigade R.F.A. From 1st Sept 1916 To 30th Sept 1916 (Volume 1)		
War Diary	Bus-Les-Artois	31/08/1916	06/09/1916

War Diary	Bertrancourt	08/09/1916	11/09/1916
War Diary	Bus-Les-Artois	12/09/1916	21/09/1916
Miscellaneous	Headquarters 184th Brigade R.F.A. Appendix 2	03/09/1916	03/09/1916
Miscellaneous	39th Divisional Artillery Order No. 33 Appendix 3	04/09/1916	04/09/1916
Miscellaneous	39th Divisional Artillery Order No. 35 Appendix 4	21/09/1916	21/09/1916
Heading	184th Brigade Royal Field Artillery October 1916		
Heading	War Diary Of 184th Brigade R.F.A. From 28/9/16 To 31/10/16 Sheets No. 4 To 19 Volume 1		
War Diary		28/09/1916	07/10/1916
War Diary	Mesnil	08/10/1916	13/10/1916
War Diary	Englebelmer	14/10/1916	31/10/1916
Heading	184th Brigade Royal Field Artillery November 1916		
Heading	War Diary Of 184th Brigade R.F.A. From 1st November To 30th November 1916 Sheets Nos. 20 & 21 Volume 1		
War Diary	Englebelmer	03/11/1916	27/11/1916
War Diary	Arneke	28/11/1916	30/11/1916
Miscellaneous	39th Divisional Artillery	26/11/1916	26/11/1916
Miscellaneous	Officers Of The 184th Brigade. R.F.A.	29/11/1916	29/11/1916
Miscellaneous	Routine Orders By Major F.E. Spencer MC Commanding 184th Brigade R.F.A.	30/11/1916	30/11/1916

(5)

WO95/2574
Mar '16 - Nov '16
184 Bde RFA

39TH DIVISION
DIVL ARTILLERY

184TH BRIGADE R.F.A.
MAR 1916-NOV 1916

BROKEN UP

39th Divisional Artillery.

Brigade disembarked HAVRE 7. 3. 16.

184th BRIGADE

ROYAL FIELD ARTILLERY.

4.2.16 TO 31st MARCH 1916

Nov 1916

184 R F A
Vol 1

Army Form C. 2118

184th Brigade RFA

WAR DIARY
INTELLIGENCE SUMMARY
(Erase heading not required.)

Instructions regarding War Diaries and Intelligence Summaries are contained in F.S. Regs., Part II. and the Staff Manual respectively. Title Pages will be prepared in manuscript.

Place	Date	Hour	Summary of Events and Information	Remarks and references to Appendices
			List of Officers	
			Head Quarters	
			Lieutenant Colonel C.M.C. RUDKIN Commanding Officer	
			Lieutenant V. HILL Adjutant	
			Lieutenant J.D. TREMLETT Orderly Officer	
			Batteries	
			A Battery — B Battery — C Battery — D Battery	
			Lieut T.W. COLES — Capt G.C. KEMP — Capt R.W. ALLEN — Major F.E. SPENCER	
			Lieut J.B. ROBERTON — Lieut F.G.H. JOHNSON — Lieut W. STRACHAN — Lieut A.W. DURRANT	
			-,- E.F. CROWDY — -,- F.D. ODELL — Lieut T.B. THOMPSON — -,- E.J.L. BENNETT	X
			-,- F. STRAKER — -,- O.N. MASH — -,- J.A. CASSERLY — -,- D.S. DOIG	
			Brigade Ammunition Column	
			Captain H.A. RAMSEY	
			Lieut M.J.R. WOOD	
			attached J.E. THOMPSON	
			A.V.W. MILES	

1st Sheet

184th Brigade R.F.A.

Army Form C. 2118

WAR DIARY or INTELLIGENCE SUMMARY

(Erase heading not required.)

Instructions regarding War Diaries and Intelligence Summaries are contained in F. S. Regs., Part II. and the Staff Manual respectively. Title Pages will be prepared in manuscript.

Place	Date	Hour	Summary of Events and Information	Remarks and references to Appendices
MILFORD	4.2.16		Orders received to prepare for service overseas	
MILFORD	6.2.16		Proceeded to LARKHILL, SALISBURY for Gun Practice, returning to MILFORD on 13.2.16	
MILFORD	21.2.16		Musketry commenced	
MILFORD	2.3.16		Musketry completed	
SOUTHAMPTON	6.3.16		Embarked on H.M.T. NIRVANA	
HAVRE	7.3.16	10.45 AM	Arrived at quay side, disembarkation completed at 3pm. Head Quarters, A & B Batteries marching to No. 5 Rest Camp, C & D and Ammunition Column going to No. 3 Rest Camp	
HAVRE	8.3.16	8.3 AM	Entrainment commenced of No. 4 Bad. The first train with HQ and A Battery leaving at 10.45 am	
THIENNES	9.3.16	6 AM	First train arrived and detrained, marched to concentration area at BLARINGHEM. The last train arriving at 7.30 pm	
BLARINGHEM	12.3.16	7.30 AM	Marched from concentration area to form the 34th Division at CROIX-DU-BAC	
STEENWERCK	12.3.16	3 pm	for a short period of instruction. Arrived and proceeded to billeting area. Reference map FRANCE Sheet 36 N.W. HQ at S.I.C.2.5, A Battery G.3.a.2.9½, B Battery A.26.d.2.9, C Battery G.2.a.1.9, D Battery G.3.d.8.1. The B.A.C. Remaining in the concentration area. Map FRANCE Sheet 36 A H & C 9.1.	
CROIX-DU-BAC	12.3.16	4 pm	Reported arrival personally at D.H.Q. and arranged for the attachment of A & B Batteries to LEFT Artillery Group, and C & D Batteries to RIGHT Group.	

Army Form C. 2118

WAR DIARY
INTELLIGENCE SUMMARY
184th Brigade RFA

(Erase heading not required.)

Instructions regarding War Diaries and Intelligence Summaries are contained in F.S. Regs., Part II. and the Staff Manual respectively. Title Pages will be prepared in manuscript.

Place	Date	Hour	Summary of Events and Information	Remarks and references to Appendices
ARMENTIES	12.3.16	6.0 pm	Personnel as follows joined Batteries in the line for instruction. Reference map BELGIUM and part of FRANCE Sheet 36 NW. Three Officers and 54 Other Ranks A/184 were attached to Batteries in the line as follows, 1 Officer & 18 Other Ranks to A/175 at I.27.6.7.2.; 1 Officer & 18 Other Ranks to B/175 at I.13.a.9.9.; 1 Officer & 18 Other Ranks at H.12.8.8.5. Three Officers and 54 Other Ranks B/184 were attached to batteries as follows, 1 Officer and 18 Other Ranks to B/175 at I.8.a.6.1; 1 Officer & 18 Other Ranks to D/160 at I.13.C.3.9. 1 Officer and 18 Other Ranks to C/160 at H.24.a.9.0. Three Officers and 47 Other Ranks C/184 were attached to Batteries as follows, 1 Officer & 16 Other Ranks to D/152 at H.22.c.7.8.; 1 Officer & 16 Other Ranks to B/152 at H.23.d.3.9.; 1 Officer & 15 Other Ranks to A/152 at H.24.C.15". Three Officers and 69 Other Ranks were attached to Batteries as follows, 1 Officer and 16 Other Ranks to B/160 at I.13.d.4.8.; 1 Officer and 17 Other Ranks to A/160 at I.13.a.7.2.; 1 Officer and 10 Other Ranks to C/152 at H.24.c.6.2.	
STEENWERCK	19.3.16		Brigade Ammunition marched into forward area and went into billets in map square A.29.b.40. arriving at 2.30 pm	
ARMENTIES	20.3.16		A/184 took over one section of Guns each from the following Batteries, A/175 B/175 & C/175 situated in the map square shewn above	

Army Form C. 2118

3rd Sheet   18th Brigade R.F.A.

WAR DIARY
or
INTELLIGENCE SUMMARY
(Erase heading not required.)

Instructions regarding War Diaries and Intelligence Summaries are contained in F. S. Regs., Part II. and the Staff Manual respectively. Title Pages will be prepared in manuscript.

Place	Date	Hour	Summary of Events and Information	Remarks and references to Appendices
ARMENTIES	20/3/16	8.30pm	B/184 brought up one section of Guns which were placed in position in map Square H 24 C 22. This battery also took over the action each of D/175 & D/160 in map Square as about C/184 took over one section of Guns from D/152 in H 24 to 7.8 D/184 took over one section of Guns from B/160 in J 13 a 4.8	
ARMENTIES	21/3/16 22/3/16		Weather mostly with some rain. No Enemy Artillery very quiet	
ARMENTIES	24/3/16	7.30pm	Orders received from HQ 39th Divisional Artillery to withdraw all personnel and guns from the firing line. The Brigade to be in readiness to march to billeting area near ST VENANT on the morning of the 26th March 1916. The withdrawal was effected and the batteries concentrated by 4.a.m on the 25th March	
ESTAIRES	25/3/16	11.40AM	The Brigade arrived at the starting point, map FRANCE Sheet 36A Open Back L 28 d 5.5 and marched via MERVILLE CORNET MALO, ST VENANT, to billeting area as follows:- HQ at P 9.6.7.0, A at P 8 C 4.3. B at P.1.d.4.2. 'C' at P.8.6.5.8. 'D' at P 7 C 16, Ammunition Column at P 2 C 0 2 Lieut A.S.BALL joined, posted to D Battery	
ARMENTIES	23.3.16			

1875 Wt. W593/826 1,000,000 1/15 T.R.C. & A. A.D.S.S./Forms/C. 2118.

WAR DIARY
INTELLIGENCE SUMMARY of 184th Brigade RFA

Army Form C. 2118

Place	Date	Hour	Summary of Events and Information	Remarks and references to Appendices
ST. VENANT	25.3.16		Lieuts E.L. BRISBORNE and S.H. MAXTED having joined and posted to A & B Batteries respectively	
ST VENANT	25.3.16 to 31.3.16		The Brigade were engaged in routine work in new billets, nothing to report.	

Charles C Pinkham
Lieut. Col.
Commanding 184th Brigade, R.F.A.

39th Divisional Artillery.

184th BRIGADE

ROYAL FIELD ARTILLERY.

APRIL 1916

5th Sheet XXXIK 18th Brigade R.F.A. Vol 2

WAR DIARY
or
INTELLIGENCE SUMMARY
(Erase heading not required.)

Army Form C. 2118

Place	Date	Hour	Summary of Events and Information	Remarks and references to Appendices
ST VENANT	1/4/16	10.0 a.m.	The Brigade was inspected by General MERCER, and in the afternoon was addressed by Brigadier General G. GILLSON, Commanding the artillery of the 39th Division – Subject – Discipline	
ST VENANT	2/4/16	2 p.m.	Two Officers and twenty N.C.O. men per battery sent to CORRE for attachment to the 121st Brigade R.F.A. 38 Division, for instruction. Remainder training for remainder of Brigade, seven Drivers found	
"	3/4/16 to 8/4/16			
"	9/4/16	4.0 p.m.	The Brigade was inspected by General MUNRO, who expressed his pleasure at what he saw	
"	10/4/16	3 p.m.	A further detachment of two officers and twenty N.C.Os, relieving the former detachment sent to attached to the 121st Brigade R.F.A., the former detachment returning to ST VENANT	
"	11/4/16		Six Riding and eleven draught horses joined the Brigade, very poor class	
"	12/4/16		The following Officers joined the Brigade and were posted to the units stated against their names. Lieut. D.A. Young B/18, Lieut R.A. Young C/18. Lieut. J.A. Young, Ammunition Column, 18th Brigade	☒

Army Form C. 2118

WAR DIARY
INTELLIGENCE SUMMARY
(Erase heading not required.)

6th Sheet   184th Brigade R.F.A.

Place	Date	Hour	Summary of Events and Information	Remarks and references to Appendices

ST VENANT	14.4.16		The 39th Division having received orders to take over the defence of the FESTUBERT-GIVENCHY Section from the 38th Division, orders were issued by the C.R.A. 39th Division for the 184 Brigade R.F.A. to take over the gun positions occupied by the 131st Brigade R.F.A. Changing gun positions with the Brigade to relieve and changing gun pits, the exchange was effected on the 14th & 15th April, and the various units occupied positions as follows:—
			
			   Head Quarters Gun Position Wagon Lines
			   A Battery F 10 d 5.6 × 13. a. 9.3
			   B " F 6 d 4.4 × 26. C. 5. 5
			   C " F 11 d 4.4 × 25 d 1.3
			   C " F 4 d 5.8 × 25 C 9.6
			   D " F 4 d 5.8 × 25 Central
			
			B. D. Batteries being brought to 6 gun establishment by the addition of half of C Battery each.
				Maps BETHUNE Enclosed Sheet 36, 36A, 36B, 36C

LOCON	16.4.16. 10am		The 184 R.F.A. became responsible for the defence of the Divisional front which extends from LA BASSEE Canal to S 22 C. 14, the 33rd Division being on the right and the 35th Division on the left	

Army Form C. 2118

WAR DIARY
or
INTELLIGENCE SUMMARY
(Erase heading not required.)

7th Sheet 184th Brigade RFA

Place	Date	Hour	Summary of Events and Information	Remarks and references to Appendices
LOCON	16.4.16		For the purpose of defence the Artillery of the 39th Division was divided into two Groups. "B" Group Commanding by Lt Col T.G.BALLARDYCE and "C" Group by Lt Col A.M.KENNARD. The Head Quarters being at F.10.6.5.2. and X.28.a.7.8 respectively. R.A. Head Quarters being at LOCON. A & C Batteries 184 Brigade R.F.A. were allotted to "B" Group and D Battery to "C" Group. Lt Col CMC RUDKIN and Lt Col KILNER taking the first Week in rest billets.	A
GIVENCHY	17.4.16		Batteries took Registration on respected targets	
"	18.4.16		A few shots were fired in retaliation for hostile shelling of our front trenches	
"	22.4.16		3 Stokes Smoke & 1 Acting Bombardier & 1 Driver Joined (Re-inforcements)	
"	25.4.16		6 Gunners Joined	
"	26.4.16		5 Gunners Joined	
"	27.4.16 4.45 AM		Ememy attack on British line at HULLUCH (500 yards South of our Sector) our batteries opened with a steady rate of fire to relieve the pressure	

PTO

Army Form C. 2118

8th Sheet 1st Brigade RFA

WAR DIARY
or
INTELLIGENCE SUMMARY
(Erase heading not required.)

Instructions regarding War Diaries and Intelligence Summaries are contained in F. S. Regs., Part II. and the Staff Manual respectively. Title Pages will be prepared in manuscript.

Place	Date	Hour	Summary of Events and Information	Remarks and references to Appendices
GIVENCHY	28.4.16	6.3 PM	S.O.S. G.A.S. Signal sent out on this Division owing to the enemy sending over clouds of gas on the line immediately south of our sector. Our batteries opened with a steady rate of fire with H.E. and this was continued until 7 pm. No Infantry attack followed.	✓

Charles B. Fisher

39th Divisional Artillery.

184th BRIGADE

ROYAL FIELD ARTILLERY.

M A Y   1 9 1 6::

Army Form C. 2118

XXXX Vol 3

WAR DIARY of INTELLIGENCE SUMMARY. 184th Brigade R.F.A.

9th Sheet

(Erase heading not required.)

Instructions regarding War Diaries and Intelligence Summaries are contained in F. S. Regs., Part II. and the Staff Manual respectively. Title Pages will be prepared in manuscript.

Place	Date	Hour	Summary of Events and Information	Remarks and references to Appendices
ESSARS	1.5.16	1.30am	Lieut T.W.Coles, "A" Battery was thrown from his horse while riding back to the Wagon Lines and sustained injuries to the base of the skull from which he died at 2.30 p.m. the same day.	
-"-	3.5.16	2pm	Lieut T.W.COLES was buried in the BETHUNE Cemetery.	
LOCON	5.5.16		Orders received from D.H.Q., R.A. by Lt.Col.C.M.C.Rudkin, ordering him to take over Command of "B" Group on the 12.5.16.	
GIVENCHY	12.5.16	10am	Lt.Col.C.M.C.Rudkin assumed command of the Artillery of "B" Group, this Group consisting of the following Batteries A/184, B/184, C/184, B/174, D/174, A/186 (Howitzer), being responsible for the defence of the Front from A.16.c.5.6½ to A.3.b.2.0 (Reference Map BETHUNE combined Sheet) and moved his Headquarters to F.10.b.5.2.	
-"-	12.5.16	9.50pm	An alarm of "Gas Attack" was received from the 33rd Division on our right and the guns of the Group opened fire at 9.51.; when the 33rd Division was asked to confirm this, it was found to be a false alarm.	
-"-	14.5.16	5am	A small mine was sprung by our Engineers at A.9.d.80.25; the Group Artillery put up a barrage to prevent the enemy occupying the Crater.	
-"-	15.5.16		A/184 moved to MAZINGHEM for one week's Mobile Training. Its place in the Group being taken by C/179.	
-"-	20.5.16	12 noon	The Artillery of the Division re-organised, Brigade Ammunition Columns abolished and the guns organised into 4 mixed Brigades of three 18 pdr Batteries and one 4.5 Howitzer Battery each; B/184 became B/186, D/184 became B/184, C/186 became D/184. "B" Group, after re-organisation, was composed of the following batteries :- C/184, A/186, B/186, C/186, D/184, B/174.	
-"-	22.5.16		A/184 returned from Mobile Training and went into Rest Billets at W.8.d.7.4.	
-"-	22.5.16	6.50pm	A small combined bombardment was carried out against the Salient at A.9.b., 2½ batteries of Artillery, Light and Medium Trench Mortars and West Machines taking part; a great deal of damage was done to the enemy trenches, and their retaliation was prompt and heavy.	

WAR DIARY

INTELLIGENCE SUMMARY — 184th Brigade R.F.A.

10th Sheet

Army Form C. 2118

Instructions regarding War Diaries and Intelligence Summaries are contained in F.S. Regs., Part II. and the Staff Manual respectively. Title Pages will be prepared in manuscript.

(Erase heading not required.)

Place	Date	Hour	Summary of Events and Information	Remarks and references to Appendices
GIVENCHY	23.5.16	8pm	D/184 took over the gun positions of D/179, this Battery forming part of "C" Group.	
LOCON	25.5.16	10am	Lt.Col.J.Allardyce took over Command of "B" Group, the Headquarters, 184th Brigade R.F.A. moving into Rest Billets at LOCON. Lt.Col.O.M.G.Rudkin proceeded on 10 days leave to ENGLAND, Major F.E.SPENCER assuming Command of the Brigade.	
LOCON	25.5.16		2/Lieut J.A.Young, A/184, 2/Lieut H.J.E.Hall, D/184 joined the Brigade and were posted to the batteries stated against their names.	
LOCON	28.5.16	10.25pm	Instructions were received that "C" Group (FESTUBERT Section) 39th Division, would be taken over by the 35th Division, and "A" Group (GUINCHY Section) 33rd Division would be taken over by the 39th Division from 10 a.m. 26.5.16. No artillery to be changed for the present.	

R.W. Allen. Capt R.F.A
for
Lieut. Col.
Commanding 184th Brigade, R.F.A.

39th Divisional Artillery.

184th BRIGADE

ROYAL FIELD ARTILLERY.

JUNE 1916

Army Form C. 2118

WAR DIARY
or
INTELLIGENCE SUMMARY
(Erase heading not required.)

XXXIX   184th Brigade RFA

11th Sheet

Vol 4

Place	Date	Hour	Summary of Events and Information	Remarks and references to Appendices
LOCON	1/6/16		A/184 took over the position occupied by C/174 at X.23.a.9.2. and moved its Wagon Line to X.13.d.2.3, coming under the orders of "C" Group Commander, (Col. Kennard) from the 1.6.16.	
LOCON	3/6/16		Lt. Col. Rudkin returned off leave.	
LOCON	6/6/16		Four Officers and 46 other ranks C/305 Brigade R.F.A., 61st Division, were attached to 184th Brigade for preliminary training on disembarkation in FRANCE	
"	11/6/16		Personnel of C/305 Brigade R.F.A. withdrawn, the Division to which they belong being ordered to take over the front held by the 38th Division.	
"	13/6/16		Orders received for the re-organization of the front held by the XI Corps, the 38th and 33rd Divisions being withdrawn, the front to be held with 3 Divisions, 33rd Division on the Right, 39th in the Centre and the 61st on the Left. To enable this to be done part of the GIVENCHY Section will be handed over to the 33rd Division on the 15.6.16, and the FERME DU BOIS Section came under the orders of the 39th Division.

The 39th Divisional Front extending from GRENIDER ROAD to OXFORD STREET inclusive with Headquarters and Advance Reports Centre as follows :-

    Headquarters.
    Right Group R. A.   LOISNE
    Left "   LACOUTURE
    Right Infantry Brigade   LOISNE
    Left   "   CENSE DU RAUX

    Advance Report Centres.
    Divisional Headquarters   LOISNE
    G.O.C., R.A.   LOISNE
    Right Infantry Brigade   S.20.c.8.2.
    Left   "   S.8.d.5.9
    Reserve "   VIEILLE CHAPELLE | |

Army Form C. 2118

WAR DIARY or INTELLIGENCE SUMMARY
184th Brigade RFA 12th Sheet
(Erase heading not required.)

Place	Date	Hour	Summary of Events and Information	Remarks and references to Appendices
LOCON	16/6/16	6 pm	Orders received that the above changes will not take place until 10 a.m. 18.6.16, and further changes in the position of batteries of this Brigade was ordered; ½ C/184 to M.34.c.3½.7, ½ C/184 to S.7.d.7½.6, D/184 to X.17.d.9.7, A/184 to S.19.b.0.8, B/184 remaining at A.4.d.4.5.	
LOCON	20/6/16	2 pm	Brigade Head Quarters moved to FOSSE CHATEAU, R.15.d.3.9.	
FOSSE	20/6/16	6 pm	The following Officers joined the Brigade and were posted as stated against their names :- 2/Lieut W.G.Grant to C/184 vice 2/Lieut R.A.Young to England sick 2/Lieut P.Fogarty to D/184 vice 2/Lieut H.J.E.Hall "	
FOSSE	24/6/16		Notification received that the British Offensive had begun, the role of the XI Corps, of which the 39th Division is part, being holding attacks.	
FOSSE	26/6/16		Orders received that an attack would be made on the enemy's trenches on the 29th and 30th over a front extending over S.10.a.& d. & S.16.a.& d. C/184 and D/184 taking part, A/184 to be in readiness to assist in barrage if the enemy attempts to counter attack across the open. Wire to be cut and parapets breached on the afternoon of the 29th, 3,060 rounds Shrapnel and 3,500 rounds H.E. is allowed for this. The main bombardment and attack to take place on the 30th at a time to be notified later.	
FOSSE	30/6/16	2am	Bombardment of Trenches commenced. After 10 minutes intense bombardment our Infantry moved to the assault, and succeeded in capturing first line and support trenches at the Boars Head. The enemy opened an intense bombardment on the captured trenches and our Infantry suffered heavy casualties and were finally forced to return to our trenches at 5.30 a.m.	

Commanding 184th Brigade, R.F.A.

39th Divisional Artillery,

184th BRIGADE

ROYAL FIELD ARTILLERY.

JULY 1 9 1 6 :

CONFIDENTIAL.

WAR DIARY

of

184th BRIGADE R.F.A.

from 1st July 1916   to 31st July 1916.

(Volume 1)

Army Form C. 2118

WAR DIARY
or
INTELLIGENCE SUMMARY

13th Sheet   184th BRIGADE RFA

(Erase heading not required.)

Place	Date	Hour	Summary of Events and Information	Remarks and references to Appendices
LA FOSSE	6/7/16		Orders received for re-organisation of the Front held by 39th Divisions CUINCHY and GIVENCHY Sections will be taken over from the 33rd Division and FERME DU BOIS Section handed over to the 61st Division. In consequence of these orders the following moves will take place on the 5th and 7th/1916. A/184 relieves B/162 at F.24.a.2½.3½ with Wagon Line at CHAMP de MARS BETHUNE. C/184 relieves A/166 at F.24.c.6.8 with Wagon Line at F.7.d.5.2. D/184 " D/166 " F.30.c.1.4 " " F.14.b.5.2 B/184 remaining at its old position at F.4.d.4.8. The Artillery of the 39th Division is organised in three Groups. FESTUBERT Left being "C" Group. Lt.Col.Kilner H.Q. at X.28.a.7.8 GIVENCHY Centre " "B" " Lt.Col.Allardyce H.Q. at F.10.b.2.4 CUINCHY Right " "Z" Group Lt.Col.Kennard H.Q. at F.23.b.3.9 The 61st Division being on the Left and the 15th Division on the Right.	
BETHUNE	9/7/16	10 am	The Headquarters 184th Brigade moved to 31, Rue Gambetta, BETHUNE.	
BETHUNE	11/7/16	12 nn	Lt.Col.C.M.C.Rudkin relieved Lt.Col.Allardyce and took command of "B" Group, moving his Headquarters to F.10.b.2.4.	
LA PEROL.	11/7/16		2/Lieut T.B. Thompson assumed the duties of Orderly Officer to Col. Rudkin.	
	13/7/16		2/Lieut R.E. Huston joined the Brigade and was posted to C/184.	
	14/7/16		2/Lieut J.E. Griffiths and two other ranks wounded.	
	15/7/16		CUINCHY Group taken over by 15th Divn. and the FERME DU BOIS Group taken over by the 39th Division from the 61st Division; at the completion of this relief the batteries of the 184th Bde. were situated as follows :— H.Q. at F.10.b.2.4. "A" Btty at M.32.c.2.9 "B" Btty at F.10.b.2.4 "C" Btty at F.4.d.4.8 & S.7.d.7½.6 "D" Btty at F.4.d.4.8.	

Army Form C. 2118

WAR DIARY or INTELLIGENCE SUMMARY

14th Sheet — 184th BRIGADE R.F.A.

(Erase heading not required.)

Place	Date	Hour	Summary of Events and Information	Remarks and references to Appendices
	16/7/16		The batteries of "B" Group subjected the enemy's trenches to an intense bombardment from 12 noon till 3.45 pm and from 10.30 pm till 3.30 am 17/7/16, retaliation fairly heavy.	
	18/7/16		The enemy's trench system was again bombarded from 2 pm till 6.30 pm, retaliation feeble.	
	19/7/16		A three hours intense bombardment of the enemy's lines was undertaken from 12 noon until 3 pm, retaliation feeble. At 11.40 pm the artillery of "B" Group co-operated with the Infantry in a small raid and fired for 1 hour 35 minutes, and again on the 22/7/16 when it fired for 20 minutes only.	
	23/7/16		Captain H.M.M. Robertson posted to 15 Wing R.F.C. as Liaison Officer and struck off the Strength.	
	24/7/16		FERME DU BOIS Group was handed over to the 31st Division; the position of the 184th Brigade after this move was as follows :—	
			Wagon Lines H.Q. F.10.b.2.4 "A" X.30.c.7.1½ X.25.c.7.9 "B" W.2.a.1.9 resting W.2.a.1.9 "C" X.24.a.0.0 X.25 central "D" X.24.c.3.6 X.19.a.2.0½	
			The 8th Division being on our Right and the 31st on our left.	

39th Divisional Artillery.

184th BRIGADE

ROYAL FIELD ARTILLERY.

AUGUST 1 9 1 6 :::

Vol 7

Confidential

War Diary
of
184th Brigade R.F.A.

From 29/7/16 to 26/8/16

(Volume I)

INTELLIGENCE SUMMARY. 184th Brigade RFA.

(Erase heading if not required.)

Instructions regarding War Diaries and Intelligence Summaries are contained in F.S. Regs., Part II. and the Staff Manual respectively. Title Pages will be prepared in manuscript.

Place	Date	Hour	Summary of Events and Information	Remarks and references to Appendices
LE PEROL	29/7/16 3/8/16		Lieut H.G.Garland joined the Brigade and was posted to "C" Battery. "B" Battery came into the line from rest and was split up into action as enfilade section at F.12.b.6.2½ and X.18.c.5.2.	
	5/8/16		B.S.M. Warner granted a temporary commission as 2/Lt. and left the Brigade on being posted to 186th.	
	6/8/16	11am	Divine Service held in the Grand Place BETHUNE and attended by O.C. & 1 Off. per battery.	
	8/8/16	10pm	1 round bombardment ordered and carried out on cross roads at S.29.d.4.7.	
	8/8/16		B.Q.M.S.J.H.Stome No. 41624 appointed a/B.S.M. & posted to B/184.	
	9/8/16		Division under orders to withdraw into Army Reserve to the area W.of the line ANCHEL – LOZINGHEM – AMLONAGNE, on being relieved by the 30th & 31st Divns	
	10/8/16		First Section withdrawn to wagons lines.	
	11/8/16	4 pm	Group control handed over to O.C. 159 Bde.R.F.A. and Brigade concentrated at AMES and BELLERY.	Map HAZEBROUCK Sheet 5A Reference LENS Sheet 11
AMES	12/8/16	5 pm	The Brigade marched to ROELLECOURT arriving at 10.30 p.m. and ordered to carry out eight days training in the MONCHY BRETON Training Area.	
ROLLECOURT	13/8/16 to 20/8/16		Battery and Brigade Training.	
	20/8/16		The Brigade was ordered to march south and take over part of the 6th Divn. Front from the river ANCRE to MARY REDAN (Q.17.a.5.3) Sheet 57D 1/20,000.	
	21/8/16	10am	Marched via MICKKKX ST.POL J DOULLENS main road to HAUTE VISSE thence to billets at GROUCHES arriving at 4.20 p.m.	
GROUCHES	22/8/16	9.15am	Marched via HALLOY – ORVILLE to billets at SARTON arriving at 11.20 a.m.	
SARTON	25/8/16		The artillery of the 39th Division was divided into two groups vide appendix I and batteries marched to their positions in the line, H.Q. 184 Bde. R.F.A. and "B" and "C" Batteries remaining at SARTON.	Appendix I attached
	26/8/16	11am	H.Q. 184 Bde.R.F.A. marched to billets at BUS-LES-ARTOIS (J.26.a.5.3) Sheet 57D 1/20,000; a/R.S.M. Gray Wheeler accidentally sustained a fracture of the leg and was evacuated to hospital.	

SECRET.   Copy No. 20

39TH DIVISIONAL ARTILLERY ORDER NO. 31.

Ref: Sheet 57D S.E.
     1:20,000   August 26th 1916.

1.   The 39th Divisional Artillery will be used in the fothcoming operations to reinforce and support the 29th Divisional Artillery.

2.   The 39th Divisional Artillery will be organised in two groups as under :-

    K Group. Commander Lt.Colonel C.H.Kilner - H.Q. Q.26.a.3.2.
        A/186 & ½C/186 - 6 guns at Q.22.c.6.3.
        B/186 & ½C/186 - 6 guns at) Q.26.d.8.3 to
        A/184   - 4 guns   ) Q.26.d.8.5.
        D/186   - 4 hows at Q.20.c.2.9
        D/179   - 4 hows at Q.20.a.2.1

    A Group Commander Lt.Colonel J.G.B.Allardyce - H.Q. Q.13.d.4.8
        A/179 & ½C/179 - 6 guns)
        B/179 & ½C/179 - 6 guns) Q.13.d.8.6
        B/174 & ½A/174 - 6 guns)   to
        C/174 & ½A/174 - 6 guns) Q.14.a.3.5
        D/174 & ½D/184 - 6 hows at Q.19.b.3.7
    In reserve B/184, C/184 and 1 Sec. D/184.

3.   The allotment to groups of O.P's in PROSPECT ROW WILL be by mutual agreement between group commanders, who will sub-allot them to batteries.

4.   Pending further orders liaison officers for battalions in the line will continue to be found by batteries of 29th Divisional Artillery who remain in direct support.

5.   Demands for ammunition will be sent to Officer i/c Dump at BERTRANCOURT.

6.   H.Q.R.A., 39th Division closes at THIEVRES at 4.0p.m. to-morrow and re-opens at ACHEUX at the same hour.

                                        s/d   B.RUSSELL
                                                Major R.A.
                                                Brigade Major
                                        39th Divisional Artillery.

Distribution:-
    Copy No. 1 - 39th Division "G".
            2 - 29th Div. Arty.
            3. - V Corps R.A.
            4. - Signals
            5 - 9 Div. Amm. Col.
          10.- 14 174th Brigade R.F.A.
          15 - 19 179th Brigade R.F.A.
          20 - 24 184th Brigade R.F.A.
          25 - 29 186th Brigade R.F.A.
          30   M.T.M'S.
          31 & 32 War Diary
          33   File.

39th Divisional Artillery,

184th BRIGADE

ROYAL FIELD ARTILLERY.

SEPTEMBER 1916

vol 7

3 guns

Confidential

War Diary

of

154' Brigade R.F.A.

From 1st Sept. 1916 to 30th Sept. 1916

(Volume 1)

Army Form C. 2118

WAR DIARY
of 184th Brigade R.F.A.
INTELLIGENCE SUMMARY Volume 1.

Sheet No. 16

(Erase heading not required.)

Instructions regarding War Diaries and Intelligence Summaries are contained in F.S. Regs., Part II. and the Staff Manual respectively. Title Pages will be prepared in manuscript.

Place	Date	Hour	Summary of Events and Information	Remarks and references to Appendices
BUS-LES-ARTOIS	31/8/16		2/Lt.R.Miller joined the Brigade and was posted to "D" Battery.	Sheet 57D S.E. 1/20,000
	1/9/16		No. 15019 a/R.S.M.Tucker E.O. joined the Brigade.	
	2/9/16		Lt.Col.Rudkin while acting as Liaison Officer to Brigadier General Hornby was wounded in the left arm but remained at duty.	
	3/9/16	5.10 a.m.	The 39th Division attacked the German front line trenches in Q.18.a & c and Q.17.b. in support of the 49th Division that were attacking EAST of the River ANCRE. The enemy's front and second line were seized and in places parties pushed on into the third line, but the trenches could not be held and by mid-day our Troops were back in our own trenches.	
	4/9/16		The following exchange of officers took place :- 2/Lieut W.G.Grant C/184 to D/184. 2/Lieut G.S.Millar D/184 to C/184.	
	5/9/16		The 39th Division took over the defence of the line from REDAN RIDGE (K.35.c.2.0) to River ANCRE and the Artillery was re-grouped in accordance with 39th D.A. Order No. 33 (appendix 2 & 3). "B" and "C" Batteries moving into the line on the night 5-6th Septr. 1916 with positions as follows :-	Appendix 2 & 3 attchd Reference Sheet 57D 1/40,000
			Gun Positions Wagon Lines B/184 Q.15.c.0.1½ C/184 Q.14.a.9.6 J.33.b.8.1½	
BERTRANCOURT	8/9/16			
	10/9/16	12.30pm	Wagon Lines shelled with 5.9 cm How; no casualties.	
	11/9/16	3pm	Wagon Lines again shelled; "A" and "D" Batteries moved to BUS-LES-ARTOIS (J.26.d.8.3).	Reference Sheet 57D 1/40,000
			"C" and "B" Wagon Lines moved to BUS-LES-ARTOIS (J.26.d.8.3).	
BUS-LES-ARTOIS	12/9/16		2/Lieut E.F.Crowdy evacuated to England sick is struck off the Strength.	
	14/9/16	10 am	Lt.Col.Rudkin relieved Lt.Col.Kilner in Command of "K" Group with H.Qrs. at P.23.c.6½.7 (ENGLEBELMER).	
	21/9/16	6 pm	The 39th Division relieved the 2nd Division and took over the whole V Corps Front, the Artillery being organised in three Groups as laid down in appendix 4. The 49th Division being on the Right and the 46th on the Left. Lt.Col.Rudkin moved his Headquarters to J.18.c.5.0 (SAILLY-AU-BOIS). and took Command of Left Group	Appendix 4 attached

Appendix 2.

S E C R E T.   U R G E N T.   R.A./51/G.

Headquarters,
    184th Brigade R.F.A. — For information.
    ———

1.   In the probable event of 39th Divisional Artillery taking over the portion of the line from REDAN RIDGE K.35.c.3.0 to R. ANCRE, the following batteries will move to-morrow evening to positions in relief of 11th Divisional Artillery, as under :—

Battery	To position	Relieving	Group.
A/179	K.32.1.2.3	C/59	)
C/179	Q.3.a.1.9	A/59	) A
B/179	Q.1.b.8.3	B/59	)
D/179	K.32.c.57.53	D/59	)

2.   Battery commanders will make all necessary arrangements for taking over, but a decision will not be arrived at by Reserve Army before to-morrow.   The relief will be made in one move.

3.   Pending other reliefs which will necessitate re-grouping the above batteries in their new positions will remain connected to Left Group H.Q. of 11th Division at Q.7.c.3.8 and O.C. "A" Group will send an officer and telephonists to that H.Q. to transmit orders etc. — Communication will be established between "A" Group and Q.7.c.3.8.

4.   The defensive zones will be those now covered by the present occupants of the positions.

5.   Guns will not be exchanged.

                                s/d   B. RUSSELL
                                        Major R.A.
                                       Brigade Major
                                    39th Divisional Artillery
3.9.16.

Appendix 3

SECRET   Copy No. 37

39TH DIVISIONAL ARTILLERY ORDER NO. 33.

Reference Sheet   September 4th 1916.
57D S.E. 1/20,000.

1. The 117th Infantry Brigade relieves the 2 battalions of 144th Infantry Brigade in the Section LONG ACRE (inclusive) – BROADWAY (exclusive) on the 6th September with H.Q. at CAPE JOURDAIN, MAILLY-MAILLET. The 118th Infantry Brigade holds from LONG ACRE (inclusive) to R. ANCRE (inclusive).

2. The 39th Divisional Artillery takes over the artillery defence of the front held by 39th Division and also of the front from BROADWAY (inclusive) to WATLING ST (Q.4.b.5.0)

3. 179th Brigade R.F.A. relieves Left Group 11th Divisional Artillery (under arrangements already notified) by sections on the nights of 4th/5th and 5th/6th and will form "W" Group 39th Divisional Artillery. The O.C. "W" Group will assume responsibility for the front BROADWAY – WATLING ST. from 6.0 p.m. on the 5th.

4. O.C. "A" Group will assume responsibility for the front BROADWAY – LONG ACRE from 9.0 a.m. on the 5th.

5. O.C. "K" Group will assume responsibility for the front LONG ACRE to R. ANCRE from 9.0 a.m. on the 6th.

6. The following moves of batteries will take place in consequence of the grouping of the Divisional Artillery (in addition to moves of 179th Brigade for which instructions have already been issued).

"K" Group (A/186   to Q.26.b.1.5½ in relief of 20th and 92nd batteries.
        (C/186

"A" Group (B/184   (from rest) to Q.15.c.0.1½ in relief of 308th battery.
        (C/184   "   "   " Q.14.a.9.6   "   "   " L Battery RHA.

7. Sections of batteries mentioned in para.6 will arrive each evening at their new positions at 7.30 p.m.

8. Ammunition will be taken over in pits as at 12 noon on the 5th (in the case of 179th Brigade) and as at 12 noon on 6th in the case of batteries relieving 26th Divisional Artillery.

9. Group Commanders will arrange for a liaison officer by night with each of the two battalions they directly support.

10. Arrangements for the relief of Medium Trench Mortars of 11th and 26th Divisions by X, Y and Z 39th Medium Trench Mortars Batteries will be made between D.T.M.O's concerned.

11. Field Survey Map boards and registration tables will be forwarded to this office for any positions vacated, and battery commanders will arrange to mark their zero lines before withdrawing aiming posts.

12. 39th Divisional Artillery assumes responsibility for each section of the front on completion of the group relief of that section.

13. H.Q.R.A. 39th Division remains at ACHEUX.

                                              s/d   B. RUSSELL
                                                    Major R.A.
                                                    Brigade Major
                                                    39th Divisional Artillery

Appendix 4

SECRET.

39TH DIVISIONAL ARTILLERY.

Ref: 1/20,000
57D N.E.
S.E.

ORDER NO. 35

1. In consequence of 6 batteries of 18-prs of 2nd Divisional Artillery being withdrawn from the line to-night, the following re-grouping of the 39th and 2nd Divisional Artillery will take place:-

Right Group.	(H.Q. 174th Bde. at P.24.d.9.1
	(A/186
	(B/186
Supporting	(B/174 and ½A/174
116th Inf.	(C/174 and ½A/174
Bde.	(D/174 and ½D/184
	(½D/184
Centre Group	(H.Q. 179th Bde. at P.6.a.5.3
	(A/179
Supporting	(B/179
116th Inf.	(D/179
Bde.	(50th, 70th and 58th (How) Batteries.
Left Group	(H.Q. 184th Bde. at J.12.c.5.0
	(A/184 and ½C/184
Supporting	(B/184 and ½C/184
117th Inf.	(C/186
Bde	(C/179
	(D/31 and 47th (How) Batteries.

2. The moves of batteries detailed in Order No. 34 issued on 19th instant are cancelled and the following substituted to take place to-night:-

(B/184 to K.31.c.6.6 in relief of 9th Battery
(½C/184

(A/184 to K.15.d.9½.7 in relief of 17th Battery
(½C/184

C/186 to K.30.c.5.3 in relief of 71st Battery.

C/179 to K.31.b.1½.1½ in relief of 15th Battery.

3. Guns will be stripped (less aiming posts and dial sights) and taken to cross roads at J.7.b.2.3 where they will be met by representatives of batteries relieved.

G.S. Wagons will be sent up to gun positions and detachments will march with them to new positions taking small stores, kits, etc. Gun limbers and G.S. Wagons have been ordered for 6.0p.m. at gun positions, from this office.

Guns will be left in pits by 2nd Div. batteries relieved.

4. Ammunition will be left in positions vacated and a guard left.

5. Batteries who have changed position or who have been attached to another group will send a runner to their new group H.Q. until communication is fully established.

OVER.

6.   H.Q. 184th Brigade will move from Rest to J.13.a.1.7.

       H.Q. 179th Brigade will move from G.7.a.3.1 to D.6.a.5.5.

       These moves to take place to-night.

       H.Q. 174th Brigade will move from Q.8.c.2.1 to Q.10.c.5.3.

       H.Q. 180th Brigade will move from Q.10.c.3.3 to Rest.

       These moves will take place at an early date to be decided by O.C. Right Group.

7.   H.Q. 39th Divisional Artillery remains at ACHEUX.

                                          s/d   B. RUSSELL
                                                Major R.A.
                                                Brigade Major
21.9.16.   39th Divisional Artillery.

39th Divisional Artillery.

184th BRIGADE

ROYAL FIELD ARTILLERY.

OCTOBER 1 9 1 6 ::

Confidential

War Diary

of

154th Brigade R.F.A

from 28/9/16 to 31/10/16.

Sheets Nos. 1/ to 19

Volume 1

WAR DIARY

Army Form C. 2118

Sheet No. 17 of 184th Brigade R.F.A. Volume I.

INTELLIGENCE SUMMARY

(Erase heading not required.)

Instructions regarding War Diaries and Intelligence Summaries are contained in F.S. Regs., Part II. and the Staff Manual respectively. Title Pages will be prepared in manuscript.

Place	Date	Hour	Summary of Events and Information	Remarks and references to Appendices
	28/9/16	6 pm	"B" Battery was ordered to move to the BEAUMONT Sector in order to reinforce A Group. Capt. David took command of C/184 and the zones of the gun of A Battery was readjusted.	
	30/9/16		Battalions of 117th Infy.Bde. holding Serre Sector is relieved by 99th Infy. Bde. On completion of relief this Bde. came under the orders of G.O.C. 39th Divn.	
	1/10/16		Battalions of 117th Infy.Bde. holding Hebuterne Sector is relieved by the 6th Infy.Bde.	
	1/10/16		The section of C/184 attached to A/184 rejoins the other section under the command of Captain David.	
	2/10/16	10 am	39th Division is transferred from the Vth to the IInd Corps and 2nd Division becomes responsible for Sector from 16 Poplars to Egg Street. H.Q. 39th Div. Arty. moved to Hedauville.	
	1/10/16	10 am	C/179 and C/186 moved out of the area and the artillery support is re-grouped with A/184, C/184 and 47th (4.5" Hows), commanded by Lt.Col.C.M.C. Rudkin forming Left Group with the zone 16 Poplars to John. Copse.	
	4/10/16		The 6th Infy.Bde. is relieved by the 152nd Highland Bde. in the Hebuterne Sector.	
	4/10/16	10 am	Owing to the readjustment of Corps Areas the wagon lines of B & D Batteries moved to Bivouacs at V.3.d.	
		6.30 pm	The 2nd Division was relieved by the 51st Highland Division and the Left Group artillery remained as before.	
	5/10/16		Capt. Allen rejoined the Brigade from England and resumed command of C/184.	
	7/10/16	9 pm	Handed over Left Group to 51st Division. A & C Batteries withdrawn to SENLIS, all W.L's moving to SENLIS at the same time.	
	8/10/16		Took over Support Group, 39th Division with H.Qrs. at MESNIL Q.28.a.9.4 A & C Batteries went into positions at Q.28.b.66.40 and Q.21.d.90.53. B Battery at Q.22.a.25.65 coming under orders of Support Group at 4.30 p.m.	Reference Sheet 57D 1/40,000
	6-9	night	Group H.Q. heavily shelled by 4.2 and gas shells. No casualties.	
	10/10/16	5 pm	Group H.Q. moved to Engle Belmer at P.24.d.60.25.	
Mesnil	10-12-13/10/16	night	All approaches to Schwaben Redoubt kept under fire by batteries of Support Group.	

Army Form C. 2118

Sheet No. 13   WAR DIARY   Volume I.

of 184th Brigade R.F.A.

INTELLIGENCE SUMMARY

(Erase heading not required.)

Place	Date	Hour	Summary of Events and Information	Remarks and references to Appendices
Englebelmer	14/9/16	2.0 pm	Support Group took part if barrage for attack on Schwaben Redoubt which was successful. Enemy barraged THIEPVAL WOOD and put intermittent rounds in HAMEL front line.	Reference Sheet 57D 1/40,000
	15/9/16	6.45 am	Captain David leaves 184th Brigade on being posted to the 46th Divisional Artillery.	
			Enemy counter-attacked at R.19.b.6.1 but was completely repulsed. Brig. Gen.Finch-Hutton remarked that due to the excellent barrage put up by the Artillery he does not think that many of the enemy escaped.	
	19/9/16	8.11 pm	Two counter attacks were made by the enemy who were unable on both occasions to penetrate the barrage formed and failed to reach our parapets. A/184s position at Q.28.b.3.2 shelled with 150 4.2 Hows. No casualties.	
	19/9/16 20/9/16	6.20 pm Noon	By order of Vth Corps 184th and 179th Brigades comes under tactical control of 51st Divisional Artillery and the following changes were made :— B/184 relieves B/174 at Q.15.c.00.15. A/184 relieves A/186 at Q.26.b.10.40. C/184 is withdrawn to Wagon Lines. D/184 remaining in its former position. By orders of CRA 51st Division 184th Bde. Batteries in action come under the tactical control of Colonel Eardley-Wilmot, whose command is to be known as No.1 Group.	
	21/9/16	10.0 am	S.O.S. sent up from Schwaben Redoubt. Enemy attacked at this point and entered our trenches at R.19.d.8.9 and 1.9, but was driven out by an immediate counter attack. 98 prisoners being captured including four officers and 2 Flammenwerfers.	
	22/9/16	12.00	All Batteries of this Group answered the S.O.S. and their fire was very effective. Enemy captured documents confirm the opinion that they consider the loss of the Schwaben as a very serious reverse.	
	21/15/16		The 39th Division attacked the STUFF Trench in co-operation with the 25th who attacked the REGINA Trench. By 5 pm all objectives were in our hands. About 400 prisoners were captured by the 39th alone. Artillery barrage was reported by everyone to be excellent. H.Q. 39th Div. Arty. moved to V.12.b.9.1.	

Army Form C. 2118

WAR DIARY Volume I.

Sheet No. 19

of 184th Brigade R.F.A.

INTELLIGENCE SUMMARY

(Erase heading not required.)

Place	Date	Hour	Summary of Events and Information	Remarks and references to Appendices
	23/9/16			
	24/9/16	12.30 p.m.	The main body 39th D.A.C. moves to area SARTON - MARIEUX. Lt.Col.C.M.C.Rudkin evacuated sick to the 2nd Highland Field Ambulance.	702
	30/9/16		Major F.E.Spencer assumed temporary command of the Brigade. 2/Lieut D.B.Reekie is transferred from "C" to "A" Battery, but is still attached to H.Qrs.	
	31/9/16		2/Lieut D.B.Reekie is detached from H.Qrs. and joins A Battery for duty.	

31/+/16

Filed for
186 184th Brigade R.F.A.

39th Divisional Artillery.

Brigade broken up 30.11.16; Batteries
divided among other Brigades of Division.

184th BRIGADE

ROYAL FIELD ARTILLERY

NOVEMBER 1 9 1 6

FINIS.

Confidential

War Diary

of

184th Brigade R.F.A.

from 1st November to 30th November
1916

Sheets Nos 20 & 21

Volume 1

WAR DIARY

Sheet No.20 of 184th Brigade R.F.A. VOLUME

INTELLIGENCE SUMMARY

(Erase heading not required.)

Place	Date	Hour	Summary of Events and Information	Remarks and references to Appendices
ENGLEBELMER	3/7/16		"C" Battery removed to area H.25.b. Also 25 horses, 1 N.C.O. and 12 men from each of the other Batteries.	Map 57 D
	9/7/16		Official information received that Lt.Col.Rutkin C.M.G. was transferred to England on the 28/X/16 from No. 14 Gen.Hsl. and is there-fore struck off the strength of the Brigade.	
	13/11/16	5.45 A.m.	The 39th Div. in conjunction with the 19th, 51st, 63rd, 2nd & 3rd Divisions attacked the enemy's lines on a three miles front and were on the whole very successful. ST.PIERRE DIVION, BEAUCOURT-SUR-ANCRE & BEAUMONT HAMEL were captured and the attack proceeds.	
		3 p.m.	Lieut Alec W.Durrant, "B" Battery, killed in action. Casualties of the Brigade for the first day of the attack also include 2 men of "A" Btty. Attack still continues; many prisoners brought in. Operations still successful.	
	14/11/16		2/Lieut E.F.Crowdy rejoins the Brigade from England, is taken on the Strength and posted to "A" Battery.	
	16/11/16	2 p.m.	"A" and "B" Batteries move up to forward position by Knightsbridge Trench, "B" at Q.16.d.2.9 and "A" at Q.16.a.9½.0.	Map Reference 57 D
	19/11/16		Received orders to pull out of positions and be in wagon lines by day-break 19th.	
	20/11/16	10 a.m.	Brigade minus "C" Battery marches through HEDAUVILLE-ACHIEUX-LOUVENCOURT-SARTON to Billets at AKPLIER.	Map Reference 57D 1/40,000
	21/11/16	9.30 a.m.	Continued march North through DOULLENS & PREVENT to Billets at CONCHY-SUR-CONCHE arriving at 6 p.m. "C" Battery marched from MARIEUX joining Bde at CONCHY.	
	22/11/16	10 a.m.	Continued march through FLENS-CROISETTE-SIRACOURT-CROIX-HERNICOURT to Billets. H.Q. "B" and "C" Batteries at HERNICOURT, "D" at WAVRON and "A" at CONTEVILLE. Brigade rested here for two days.	
	25/11/16 26/11/16	10 a.m.	Continued march to WESEREHEM. Continued march through AIRE to Billets at BOESINGHEM arriving at 1.45 p.m.	Map Ref 1473 36/NE 1/40,000
CANEUF	27/11/16	9 a.m.	Continued march through HAZEBROUCK to ARNEKE arriving at 5 p.m.	Appendix 5
	28/11/16 and 29th		Continued march through MISCELLANY and at D.S.O.(Reserve) 198. Section of Brigade which was done on the 28th and 29th. See Appendix 5.	

Army Form C. 2118

Sheet No. 21   **WAR DIARY**   Volume 1

of 184th Brigade R.F.A.

INTELLIGENCE ~~**SUMMARY**~~

(*Erase heading not required.*)

Instructions regarding War Diaries and Intelligence Summaries are contained in F. S. Regs., Part II. and the Staff Manual respectively. Title Pages will be prepared in manuscript.

Place	Date	Hour	Summary of Events and Information	Remarks and references to Appendices

ARNEKE	30/11/16	Mdt.	By order of 39th Div. Arty. the transfer of batteries of 184th Brigade R.F.A. took place.
			 A/184 6 gun battery 18-prs. commanded by Capt. R.W.Allen to 174th Bde.
			 B/184 6 gun battery 18prs " Major F.E.Spencer to 186th Bde.
			 D/184 4 gun battery 4.5"Hows " Capt. A.C.Hancocks to 179th Bde.
			
			 The H.Q. of 184th Brigade R.F.A. remains as a unit pending further instructions.
			
			 2/Lieut A.J.Marriott & 2/Lieut D.A.Young transferred to 39th D.A.C. Major F.E.Spencer MC R.A. relinquishes command of the 184th Brigade.
			
			                               F.S.Spencer
			                                  Major RA
			                          Commanding 184th Bde. RFA	

SECRET   39TH DIVISIONAL ARTILLERY   R.A./48/G

(1)   In accordance with G.H.Q. O.B./818 of 23.8.1916 the present 4 brigades of 39th Divisional Artillery will be re-organized into 3 brigades.

       174th Brigade will consist of 3 six gun 18-pr batteries
                                     1 six gun 4.5"How battery
       186th Brigade will consist of 3 six gun 18-pr batteries
                                     1 six gun 4.5"How battery
       179th Brigade will consist of 2 six gun 18-pr batteries
                                     1 four gun 4.5"How battery
       184th Brigade will cease to exist

(2)   In accordance with G.H.Q. O.B./1866 of 16.11.1916 divisional artilleries will be reduced to 2 brigades (174th and 186th) constituted as above and 179th Brigade will become surplus, available for the formation of "Army brigades" of which there will be 2 in the VIII Corps.

(3)   The first step will be the formation of 6 gun batteries as follows :-

       1 Section C/174 will join A/174
       1 Section C/174 will join B/174
       1 Section C/179 will join A/179
       1 Section C/179 will join B/179
       1 Section C/184 will join A/184
       1 Section C/184 will join B/184
       1 Section C/186 will join A/186
       1 Section C/186 will join B/186
       1 Section D/184 will join D/174
       1 Section D/184 will join D/186

(4)   Thus all C Batteries (as at present constituted) will cease to exist and also D/184.

(5)   As soon as the 6 gun batteries are formed the following batteries (as then constituted) will be transferred as follows :-

       A/184 becomes C/174
       B/184 becomes C/186
       H.Q. 184th Brigade becomes surplus.

(6)   The 39th Divisional Ammunition Column will be re-organized as follows :-

       A Echelon will consist of the present 1 & 2 Sections to be reconstituted as shown in the appendix.

       The present number 3 section will become surplus and will be available to form an Army Artillery Brigade Ammunition Column of which there will be two in the VIII Corps.

       B Echelon remains as at present less the personnel, horses and vehicles withdrawn as shown in appendix. It will be re-numbered No.3 Section.

                                                             OVER

-2-

(7) All personnel and equipment of batteries ceasing to exist (see para. 3) will be transferred with the sections to which they now belong.

(8) Re-organization as above will commence on 28th instant. Brigades and Divisional Ammunition Column will report completion as early as possible.

(9) Brigades and Divisional Ammunition Column will render as soon as possible after re-organization, a return (on pro forma attached) showing transactions in connection with the same.

(10) All surplus personnel etc. will be retained on the strength of the unit pending further instructions.

(11) The posting of Battery Commanders and seconds in command are shown in the appendix.

Battery commanders of 6 gun batteries may retain 5 subaltern officers, viz., 3 section commanders and 2 surplus. All other officers becoming surplus in consequence of re-organization will be transferred to the Divisional Ammunition Column.

Brigades will render a list showing postings of subaltern officers and names of officers transferred to Divisional Ammunition Column, at the same time as the return mentioned in para. 9.

Brigade Commanders will notify Officer Commanding, Divisional Ammunition Column of the names of officers they intend to transfer at least 24 hours in advance of the officers joining.

(12) Appendices attached :-
    B. Distribution of Brigade H.Q.
    C. Composition in detail of a 6 gun battery (18pr or 4.5")
    D. War establishment of units of Divisional Artillery on re-organization (personnel and transport).
    E. List of Battery Commanders and seconds in command.
    F. Old and new designations of units.
    G. Return showing transactions in connection with re-organization.
    H. Composition in detail of Section A Echelon D.A.C.
    I. War Establishment of Army Artillery Brigade Ammunition Column.

                                                s/d B. RUSSELL
                                                   Major R.A.
                                               Brigade Major
26.11.1916.   59th Divl. Artillery

OFFICERS OF THE 184th BRIGADE R.F.A.

		Unit	Remarks
Adjt. Lt. V. Hill	(R)	H.Q.	Remains as Adjt. 184th R.F.A.
O.O. 2/Lt. T. B. Thompson	(T)	H.Q.	Posted to "B" Battery
T/Capt. W. Strachan	(R)	"A"	Second in Command to "A" Battery
2/Lieut J. A. Young	(SR)	"A"	No change
2/Lieut W. B. Reekie	(TF)	"A"	" "
2/Lieut J. B. Roberton	(T)	"A"	" "
2/Lieut A. J. Marriott	(SR)	"A"	To D.A.C.
2/Lieut E. F. Crowdy	(R)	"A"	To H.Q. 184th Bde. as O.O.
Major F. E. Spencer MC	(R)	"B"	No change
T/Capt. H. A. Ramsey	(T)	"B"	" "
2/Lieut D. S. Doig	(T)	"B"	" "
2/Lieut E. J. Bennett	(T)	"B"	" "
2/Lieut A. S. Ball	(T)	"B"	" "
Capt. R. W. Allen	(R)	"C"	To command A/184
T/Lt. H. G. Garland	(T)	"C"	To B/184
2/Lieut R. E. Huston	(SR)	"C"	To A/184
2/Lieut J. A. Casserly	(R)	"C"	To A/184
2/Lieut D. A. Young	(SR)	"C"	To D.A.C.
Capt. A. C. Hancocks	(R)	"D"	No change
Lieut D. M. L. Johnston	(R)	"D"	" "
2/Lieut W. Jones	(SR)	"D"	" "

                                                        s/d   F. E. SPENCER
                                                               Major RA
29/11/16.   Commanding 184th Bde. R.F.A.

ROUTINE ORDERS

BY

MAJOR F. E. SPENCER MC COMMANDING 184th BRIGADE R. F. A.

30th November 1916.

POSTINGS.   The undermentioned transfers take place with effect from 30th November 1916.

    L. 38440 Dvr. J. E. Sparkes   From Bde. H. Q. to 186th Bde
    L. 38430 Dvr. E. C. Weaver   From Bde. H. Q. to R. A. H. Q.
    L. 40231 Dvr. G. Presko   From Bde. H. Q. to B/184

REORGANIZATION.

Batteries of the 184th Brigade will come under the Command of the Brigades to which they are allotted on re-organization from 12 midnight 30th Novr – 1st Decr.

184th Brigade ceases to exist from midnight 30th Novr – 1st Decr.

Brigade Headquarters remain intact as a unit pending further instructions.

Major F. E. Spencer MC ceases to command the Brigade with effect from 1st December 1916.

APPOINTMENTS.

Bo. L. 38337 Corpl. J. Wood is appointed Acting Sergt. (vice Sergt. Armes evacuated) ith effect from 29/11/16.

                     s/1   THOS B. THOMPSON
                              2/Lieut
                         for Adjutant
                    184th Brigade R. F. A.

www.ingramcontent.com/pod-product-compliance
Lightning Source LLC
Chambersburg PA
CBHW081245170426
43191CB00037B/2052